EOE/CH

We hope you enjoy this

DIGITAL 101

By Ben Hubbard   Illustrated by Diego Vaisberg

FRANKLIN WATTS

LONDON•SYDNEY

CONTENTS

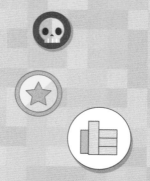

BECOMING A DIGITAL CITIZEN

WHAT IS DIGITAL CITIZENSHIP?

When we log onto the internet we become part of a giant, online world.

In this world we can use our smartphones, tablets and computers to explore, create and communicate with billions of different people. Together, these people make up a global digital community. That is why they are known as digital citizens. When you use the internet you are a digital citizen too. So what does this mean?

CITIZEN VS DIGITAL CITIZEN

A good citizen is someone who behaves well, looks after themselves and others, and tries to make their community a better place. A good digital citizen acts exactly the same way. However, the online world is bigger than just a local neighbourhood, city or country. It spans the whole world and crosses every kind of border. It is therefore up to all digital citizens everywhere to make this digital community a safe, fun and exciting place for everyone.

MY DIGITAL FUTURE

Digital technology is how we manage our lives in the modern world. Many people stay logged-in to the internet, their networks and the wider online community using mobile and wearable devices. Keeping up-to-date with trends in digital technology is an important part of being a digital citizen. The future, after all, will be digital. But what developments might this bring? This book explores the world of digital technology today and how it might look tomorrow.

DID YOU INVENT THAT? WHAT IS IT?

A TRANSPORTER THAT TAKES ME TO ANY PLACE I SEE ONLINE. I'M OFF TO VISIT THE DINOSAURS.

WON'T THAT BE DANGEROUS?

THAT'S WHY I'VE ALSO INVENTED THIS FLYING INVISIBILITY BUBBLE. IT'S BITE-PROOF!

CONNECT, COLLECT AND COMMUNICATE

Can you imagine life without the internet?

The internet is how we communicate using messages written out in text. It is how we collect information from websites. It is where we go to listen to music, watch films, play games, read news and do our shopping. For digital citizens, the internet is part of everyday life.

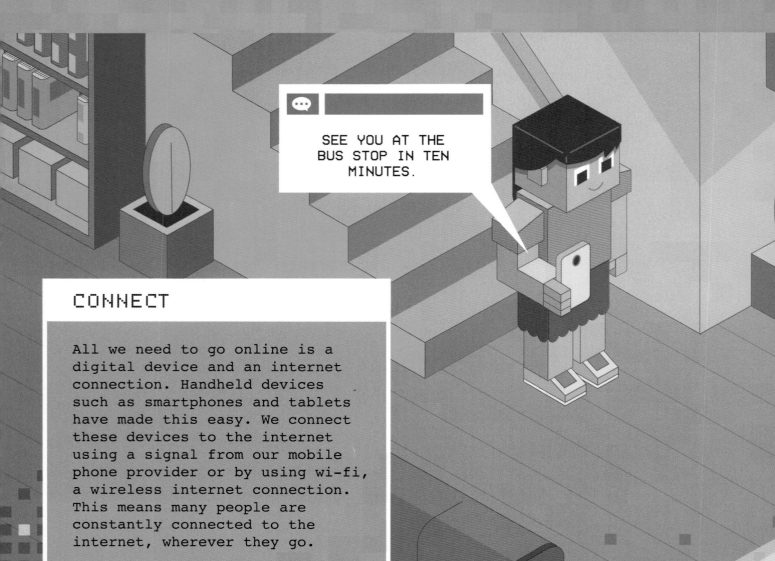

SEE YOU AT THE BUS STOP IN TEN MINUTES.

CONNECT

All we need to go online is a digital device and an internet connection. Handheld devices such as smartphones and tablets have made this easy. We connect these devices to the internet using a signal from our mobile phone provider or by using wi-fi, a wireless internet connection. This means many people are constantly connected to the internet, wherever they go.

COLLECT INFORMATION

The internet has made finding information easier than at any time in history. In a few clicks we can find a bus timetable, look at a weather forecast and see what's on TV. It's also very helpful for homework!

COMMUNICATE

Having a handheld digital device that is constantly connected has changed the way we communicate. Now we can have almost instant access to friends and family by making a video call or sending them an email, social media message or instant message. Sometimes it seems many of us spend more time messaging each other than talking.

SEND ME A TEXT IF YOU'LL BE LATE HOME FROM SCHOOL.

CAN YOU FORWARD THAT EMAIL FROM DAISY TO ME?

GRAN SAYS SHE'LL SKYPE TONIGHT AT 7.

TRUSTED HELP

It is always a good idea to have a trusted adult around when you go online.

They can help you set up your social media accounts, screen name and avatar. They can also show you how to navigate the internet and avoid websites that aren't good for kids. Most importantly, your trusted adult is a 'go-to' person if something goes wrong.

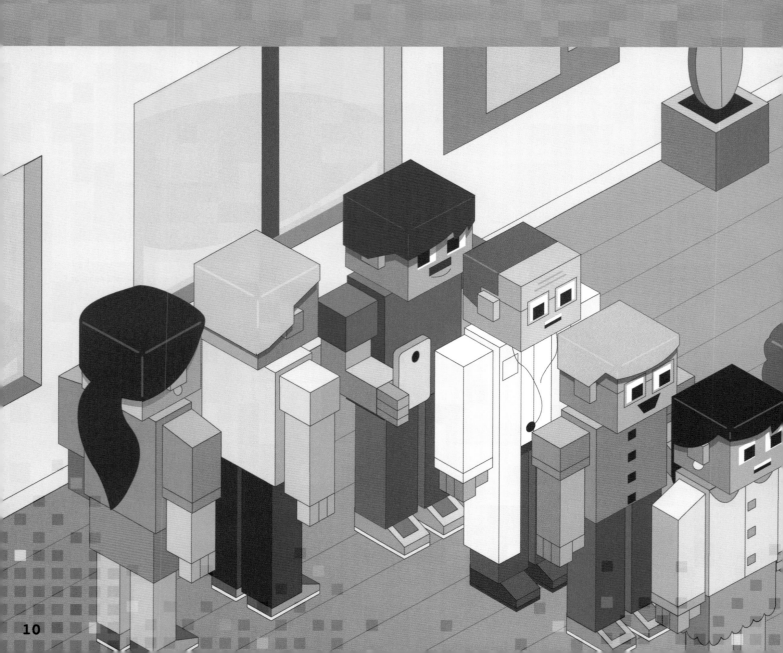

WHICH ADULT TO CHOOSE?

Choosing the right trusted adult is an important step. It could be a parent, carer or other grown-up family member that lives at home. However, it's best to have a trusted adult that knows more about the online world than you. Otherwise, you will end up being their trusted adult!

> NOW GRANDAD, HOW WILL YOU KEEP ME SAFE ON THE INTERNET?

> IS THE INTERNET THAT THING WITH EMAIL?

ONLINE IDENTITY

To avoid giving away too much about yourself, it is best to have a screen name and avatar for your online accounts. A screen name is just a nickname and can be anything you like. Some mix up a favourite singer's name with numbers and symbols, for example. An avatar is the online face that you show to the world. Many people copy and paste the face of a movie star or animated character for this.

PASSWORDS AND PASSCODES

Passwords are how we protect our online accounts, such as email or social media.

This stops anyone else gaining access and acts as our main line of protection. A second line of protection is a passcode, which is like a password for our digital devices. This means that even if your phone, tablet or computer is stolen, a thief can't access the information it contains.

PASSCODES

Passcodes are passwords usually made up of numbers that we use to access our digital devices. Without the correct passcode, the device stays on its lock screen. Some digital devices disable completely after a certain number of incorrect guesses. Phones and tablets often come with a fingerprint scanner to unlock a device instantly.

PICKING A PASSWORD

A password is a combination of letters, numbers and special characters that only you know. As a rule, the longer the password, the harder it is to crack. If possible, passwords over 12 characters are best. Try mixing up some different numbers and letters and using upper and lower case too. But make sure it is something you will remember! Eight-year old Jenny has picked this password:

1

Oito
(eight in
Portuguese)

PASSWORDS

A strong password is your best defence against somebody trying to access your online accounts. Websites such as social media sites ask you for a password every time you log in. Only your trusted adult should know what your passwords are and you must never write them down. It's also important to log out when you have finished, especially if you have used a device other people have access to.

MY MOBILE'S BEEN STOLEN!

DID IT HAVE A PASSCODE PROTECTING IT?

YES, AND I'VE ALREADY BEEN ONLINE TO CHANGE ALL OF MY PASSWORDS ON MY SOCIAL MEDIA ACCOUNTS.

GOOD, THAT'LL HOPEFULLY STOP ANYONE HACKING INTO YOUR ACCOUNTS. NOW LET'S CONTACT YOUR MOBILE PROVIDER AND THE POLICE.

2 MAS (the name of her dog, Sam, backwards in capitals)

3 1973 (The year her favourite uncle was born)

4 ****** (six stars for Jenny's age when she got Sam)

5 = OitoMAS1973******

PROTECTING PERSONAL DETAILS

In the real world we would not go around giving out our personal information to strangers in the street.

The online world is the same. But what does our personal information include? And how do we know what is private and what we can make public?

PERSONAL INFORMATION

Your personal information is made up of the things that identify you. This usually includes your:
- Full name
- Address
- School
- Telephone numbers
- Email address
- Family and friends' personal information

PUBLIC INFORMATION

There is lots of information that doesn't reveal your identity and is safe to give out online. Otherwise you wouldn't be able to say anything! Examples of information that is OK to make public includes your:

- Opinions. It's OK to make your opinions public if you are respectful of others
- Favourite food, singer or sports team
- How many brothers and sisters you have
- Places you'd like to visit on holiday
- What you'd like to do as a job

WELCOME TO THE WEB

A WORLD OF WEBSITES

Websites are where we go to discover new things, read about our favourite subjects and fill our heads with facts.

For example, did you know there are over two billion websites in the online world? With so many options, how do we know which are safe for kids to visit?

WHAT IS A WEBSITE?

Each website is made up of a collection of web pages. Every time we click on a web page, packets of information from the website are sent to our computer. But often we don't know who is controlling the website. This means we have to be careful about trusting what we read.

IT SAYS HERE SHE'S 19.

AND HERE IT SAYS 17.

YOU'RE BOTH WRONG. SHE'S 36.

CHOOSE BEFORE YOU CLICK

Clever digital citizens get their information from trustworthy websites. The suffix, or three letters at the end of a website, is the first clue to what it is about. These show you if the website is there to provide information, make money or has an unspecified purpose. The most common suffixes are:

1 .edu — an educational institution, such as a school or university

WHICH WEBSITE IS ALRIGHT?

Not all websites are right for kids. Some have sex, violence or upsetting content. Others are fake sites that are designed to scam or steal from people. Clever digital citizens choose which websites they visit.

The simplest way to find kid-friendly sites is to get a list from your school. The other way — you guessed it — is to go online. The following sites contain lists of dozens of websites for kids only. Check them out:
https://www.commonsensemedia.org/lists/kid-safe-browsers-and-search-sites
https://www.todaysparent.com/family/30-fun-and-safe-kids-websites/
http://www.kidsites.com

IF YOU GET YOUR INFORMATION FROM SOCIAL MEDIA SITES AND BLOGS IT'S OFTEN INCORRECT. TRY THIS ENCYCLOPEDIA WEBSITE. IT SAYS THE POP STAR IS 21.

2 .gov — a government website

3 .org — usually a non-profit site, such as a charity

4 .com — a commercial site that is designed to make money

5 .net — a website without a specified purpose

CYBER SEARCHING

Only 30 years ago people found most of their information using books, magazines and newspapers.

Doing homework often meant a visit to the local library. Today, information about almost anything is only a few clicks away. However, we have to be careful about where we look.

SAFE SEARCHING

Searching the internet is fantastic fun, but it pays to have a trusted adult around when you do it. They can help you decide what key words to type into your search engine and set up filters that block out any website nasties. There are also search engines just for kids such as:
http://www.safesearchkids.com
http://www.kiddle.co
http://www.kidzsearch.com
http://www.swiggle.org.uk

As well as kid-friendly search engines, there are also child versions of some adult websites. Some of these are:
http://kids.britannica.com/
https://kids.youtube.com
http://www.natgeokids.com/

YOU CAN FIND ALMOST ANYTHING ON THE INTERNET TODAY.

ELEPHANTS FLYING AEROPLANES: 2,040,00 WEB PAGES!

SMALLEST SAXOPHONE IN THE WORLD: 1,720,000 WEB PAGES.

KEY WORDS

Using a few key words will get you to the best information fast. You don't need to type full sentences. Try typing the highlighted key words from this sentence into a kid-friendly search engine: What is the longest river in Africa?

WEBSITE CHECK

Did you know you can check out a website before you even click on it? You can do this by putting the website's name into a search engine and adding 'reviews'. This can show if anyone has had trouble with it in the past. Remember that if you end up on a website that you don't like for any reason, you can just click out.

WHY ARE SOME OF THESE WEBSITES BLOCKED?

BECAUSE THEY HAVE NASTY STUFF THAT MIGHT UPSET YOU.

FAIR ENOUGH, I'VE ALREADY SEEN SOME STUFF I DON'T LIKE!

SOCIAL SOCIETY

How do you connect with other people online?

Do you use social media, or are you a gamer? Are you a hobbyist with special interests, or a text-talker who loves forums, chat rooms, instant messaging and microblogging? Perhaps you are not sure what these things are. Don't worry: they are all explained here.

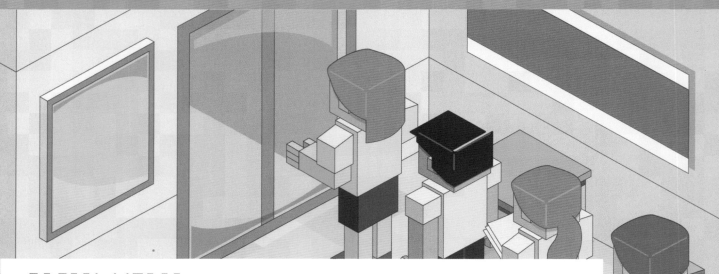

SOCIAL MEDIA

Websites and apps that allow people to share posts, photos and videos are known as social media. Social media sites are usually free, but they require users to register and log-in to use them. Many people stay in touch with friends and family on social media sites and meet new people there too.

GAMING

Playing games over the internet, often against multiple players, is known as gaming. Gamers play against others from all over the world and can interact with them by sending messages or chatting live over headsets. Often, a large network of people is formed around a single popular game.

TEXT-TALKERS

Internet forums are traditional discussion websites where people have online text conversations about particular topics. Forums are not live, unlike chat rooms, instant messaging and microblogging websites and apps. People use these websites and apps on their phones, tablets and computers to chat and give their opinions in real time.

HOBBYISTS

Hobbyist websites are for people who share a passion for a particular hobby or interest, from crafting to birdwatching to miniature model-making. Often a hobbyist website includes its own forum or chat room, and links to helpful websites.

MY NETWORKS

Did you know hundreds of millions of young people have a social media account?

Many social media sites are just for children, but young people can also often join adult social media sites too. Some of these sites say their members must be at least 13 years of age, but others have no restrictions. So how do you know if you're old enough to join and how should you stay safe in the social media world?

TRUSTED TALK

Talking to a trusted adult about joining an adult social media site is the best first step. If they think you're too young for a particular site, they can help you find one that is more suitable. Make your trusted adult one of your 'friends', so they can help you along the way.

PRIVACY SETTINGS

Once you've agreed on a social media site, your trusted adult can help you with its privacy settings. These control who can see your posts, blogs, videos and photos. Choosing a 'friends only' privacy setting is best. Make sure to check the privacy settings regularly, as websites sometimes change their policies.

PAUSE BEFORE POSTING

Even with a privacy setting of 'friends only', others may be able to see what you post on social media. It's therefore important not to post anything that may upset or embarrass you, or anyone you know. Such posts might include a silly photo, or a comment that could hurt someone's feelings. A quick pause to think before you post can help prevent you uploading something you'll later regret.

I WONDER HOW I CHANGE THE PRIVACY SETTINGS ON THIS?

BY CLICKING HERE AND HERE. AND YOU CAN UPLOAD YOUR AVATAR HERE. SEE?

RESPECT OTHERS

Good digital citizens always respect others on social media. This means being polite, friendly and kind. If someone is not behaving this way towards you, you can block them from your social media account.

STAY SECRET

It's important not to post anything that gives away your personal information, or that of your friends. Personal information includes your name, phone number and address. You can also use a screen name and avatar for your account to protect your identity.

HOBBIES AND INTERESTS

Have you ever felt like you were the only person in the world that liked a particular thing, such as a certain toy, book or film?

In the online world there is almost certainly someone who likes it just as much as you! This is why the internet is a great place to unite people with specific hobbies, subjects and interests. It can help new people become interested too.

WHICH WEBSITE?

There are a vast number of websites online dedicated to a specific subject, hobby or interest. These can be about almost anything — from slot-car racing to arcade games from the 1980s. Websites can also be run by a group dedicated to a particular thing, called a club or association. It's usually easy to become a member, but always check with your trusted adult first.

STAY IN TOUCH?

Websites dedicated to a particular interest or hobby often keep in touch with their members through email newsletters. Sometimes these are nice things to receive. At other times there may be too many emails, or your email address may be passed on to other people. For this reason, it is important not to give out your email address unless you are sure how it will be used.

BEWARE THE BILL

It's easy to spend money on 'extras' on websites dedicated to a special hobby. Before you agree to purchasing anything, make sure you have your trusted adult's consent. The simplest thing is to never fill out any bank details on a website or agree to anything that might cost money.

THEY SAY THIS TROMBONE OIL IS GREAT STUFF. CAN I BUY SOME?

BUT YOU DON'T OWN A TROMBONE.

WEIRD AND WONDERFUL ONLINE HOBBIES

ToyVoyagers — a website that sends your stuffed toy on trips around the world and posts photos of their adventures.

Extreme Ironing International — a group that carries out ironing in strange and difficult situations, like mountain climbing or kayaking through rapids. The results are then posted online.

Soap Carving — a hobby often picked up by people at home who then post their soap carvings online.

GAMING GROUPS

Gaming websites are exciting places where you can enjoy the action with players from around the world.

However, they are more than just play areas. They are also places you can interact with others who love the same games as you. This is why online gaming makes up one of the largest networks of the internet. Staying safe and protected while you are gaming is therefore key.

THIS IS AWESOME. IT'S LIKE ANOTHER WORLD!

LOADS OF THE SAME PEOPLE SHOW UP HERE EVERY WEEK.

WHICH GAME?

Online games aren't all first-person shooters or quest games. There are also sports, strategy, fitness and family games that require a range of different playing skills. Have a look around online to find some games you can play with your trusted adult or others at home.

BLOCK THE BULLY

Bullying can happen in gaming, just as it does in the real world, in the form of nasty messages or even threats from other players. 'Griefing' is a form of bullying where other players harass you or destroy things you have built in an online game. The simplest way to deal with these bullies is to block them, or change the game's settings so only people you know can join in with you.

WHAT DOES HE WANT?

HE SAYS HE'S GOT A BOOK ABOUT GAMING HE CAN SEND ME.

BEST NOT TO TRUST HIM. HE COULD BE ANYONE.

PERSONAL PRIVACY AND PREDATORS

Gaming sites require users to have a screen name and avatar to protect their personal identity. It's also important never to give away details about yourself or your location. Sometimes predators can target children through online gaming. If someone is being extra nice to you, asking you lots of questions and offering things for free, it is best not to trust them. Block them if they persist.

EXPLAINING THE WORLD

Blogs, instructional videos, video blogs (vlogs) and podcasts (digital spoken word files) are an excellent way to learn from the experts online.

These can give us information about how things work, or hands-on advice on building things. They can also provide us with walkthroughs of online games and reviews of the latest technology. They can help us become both capable digital citizens and also informed consumers.

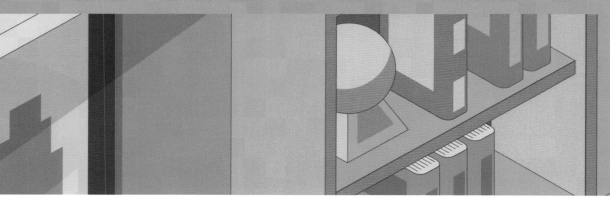

HOW TO DO IT...

Have you ever dreamed about making a smartphone projector? Or perhaps a simple robot? It's easy to learn how with instructional videos. Simply type what you'd like to make into a video-sharing website or a general search engine.

USEFUL REVIEWS

Part of being a smart digital citizen is staying informed about the latest digital technology and what it promises to do. It's easy to find reviews on a new product by entering its name and 'review' into a search engine. Reviews often show that the latest thing isn't what it's cracked up to be, which can save you a lot of money and heartache.

GAME WALKTHROUGHS

All gamers know the frustration of being defeated at a difficult point in a game — over and over and over again. Walkthroughs of video games can help immensely with these tricky bits. They can also offer cheats if you've really had enough of doing it the honest way. Simply drop your game's name and 'walkthrough' or 'cheat' into a search engine.

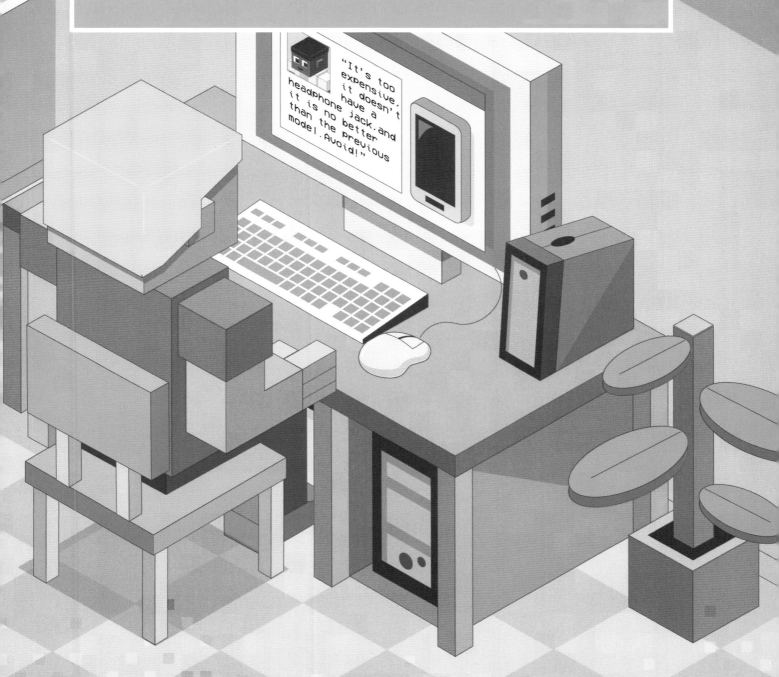

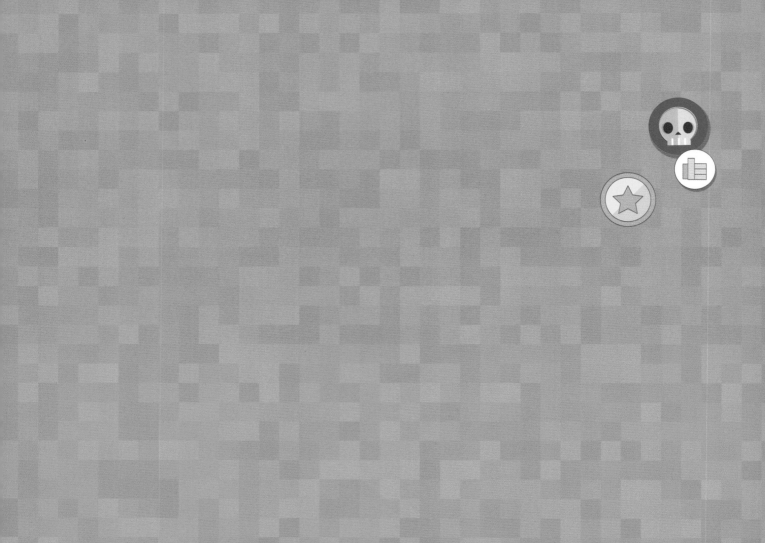
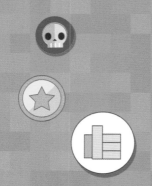

GOOD NETIQUETTE

WHAT IS NETIQUETTE?

Being a good digital citizen means treating people online as you do in the real world.

However, sometimes it's difficult in the online world to express what you mean. It's easy for misunderstandings to happen by accident. This is why you have to work harder in the online world to show you mean well and are being courteous and polite.

WE'RE GOING TO KILL YOU AT THE GAME TODAY.

HUH?!

WHAT IS NETIQUETTE?

Netiquette is made up of the two words 'etiquette' and 'net', for the internet. Etiquette means the rules for behaving well. Here are some netiquette rules to follow:

1 Don't SHOUT by typing in capital letters.

2 Don't trade insults with people, which is known as 'flaming'.

AVOID MISUNDERSTANDINGS

When we talk to people in the real world, it's easy to make them understand us. Sometimes the way we say something or how we use our body language can show others whether we are joking or being serious. But online, we do not have access to these visual clues. Therefore, it's best to explain if you are being sarcastic or making a joke. You can easily do this by adding some emojis at the end of your sentence, or text clues such as ;-).

I MEAN: WE'RE GOING TO KILL YOU AT THE GAME TODAY!

3 Check before you click, to make sure what you are saying is clear.

4 Respect the privacy of others.

5 Share your knowledge and help newbies if they don't know the rules.

TO SHARE OR NOT TO SHARE?

For most of the last century people had to write a letter to tell others what they'd been up to.

Now we can post every aspect of our daily lives instantly to our social media accounts. However, what is appropriate information to share and how do we know if we are sharing too much?

TOO MUCH INFORMATION

We all know people who seem glued to their social media accounts. Every day there are dozens of posts, photos and microblogs about what they are doing and how they are feeling. Sometimes it can become a bit too much. Every digital citizen has the right to post whatever they want online. But sometimes it's also good to pause before you post and ask yourself the question: 'Is this really worth sharing with others?'

SO? WHAT HAPPENED?

HE CHOSE HAM AND CHEESE.

SHARING SAFELY

To share safely with people on social media the first priority is to protect our personal information. This includes details about our future plans that could be used against us. For example, writing a post about an upcoming holiday that includes the dates you will be away is like telling the world that your house will be empty during that time. It's also important not to post details of where you are going to be on a particular day. You don't know who the information could be forwarded on to.

PHONE ETIQUETTE

In the modern world, many of us are constantly glued to our smartphones and tablets.

Instead of talking to each other, we often send a message instead. Clever digital citizens use their digital devices as communication tools — not to replace real interactions. Here are some guidelines for good 'phone etiquette'.

RESPECT THE LIVING

When you are with someone else, keep your texting, messaging and phone calls to a minimum. Otherwise it's like telling your companion they are less important than everyone else.

TRY TALKING, NOT TEXTING

Messaging is a great way of keeping in touch, but long messaging conversations can be time consuming and unnecessary. Sometimes a short phone call is the simplest option. It also means you are interacting with a live person!

SWITCH IT OFF

There are some places where even a phone on silent mode can be irritating for others around us. These include places like dark cinemas, or at the family dinner table. Using your phone in the classroom is almost always a bad idea! Good digital citizens learn when to switch their phones off and be considerate of other people.

SEE THE GAME?

DING DING

YEP. THAT'S IT FOR ARSENAL.

BZZT! BZZT!

SHALL WE GO IN NOW?

VZZZZZT

BUT WE'LL HAVE TO STOP TEXTING!

PHONE PRIVACY

Talking loudly on your phone, having alerts that go off all the time, or playing music in public is not good phone etiquette. In these situations, it is best to keep conversations short and plug in your headphones.

MESSAGING AWARE

Emails and instant messaging are the main method of communication for many of us.
Even if your phone and tablet are on silent mode you can still message your friends. And once you've read the message you can delete it forever, right? Wrong. Everything we do online lives on in cyberspace.

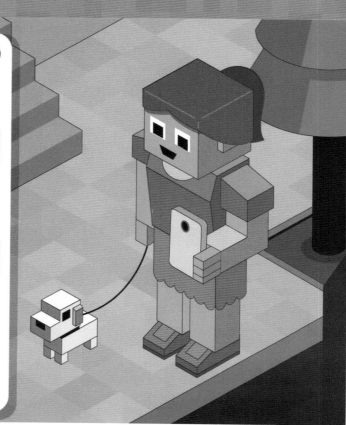

ME
MR HUMPHREYS IS SOOO BORING. AND HE SMELLS.

SUE
AND DID YOU SEE HIS AWFUL TIE TODAY?

ME
I DIDN'T DO ANY HOMEWORK LAST NIGHT. CAN'T BE BOTHERED.

SUE
MIND YOUR DAD DOESN'T FIND OUT.

ME
HE LETS ME DO WHAT I WANT. LEAST I'M NOT A SWOT LIKE JESS.

SUE
I KNOW. MUST BE BORING TO BE SOOO BRAINY.

DIGITAL FOOTPRINT

Everything you do online leaves a trail called a digital footprint. Your digital footprint is a record of your internet activity. It shows what you searched for, which websites you visited, what you wrote in messages and what you posted. Your digital footprint can only be seen by computer experts but it is a permanent record: once it is put down it is almost impossible to remove.

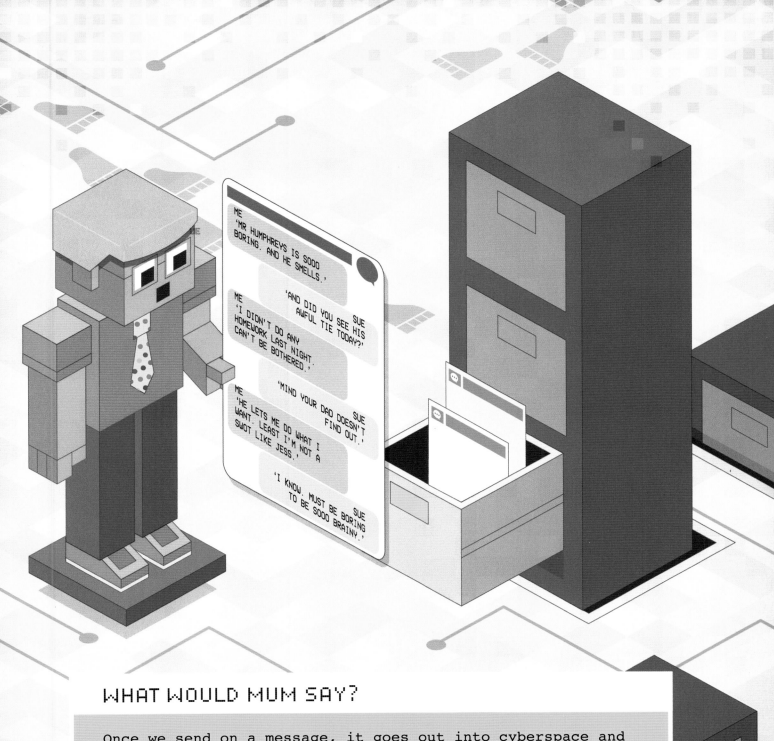

ME
'MR HUMPHREYS IS SOOO
BORING. AND HE SMELLS.'

SUE
'AND DID YOU SEE HIS
AWFUL TIE TODAY?'

ME
'I DIDN'T DO ANY
HOMEWORK LAST NIGHT.
CAN'T BE BOTHERED.'

SUE
'MIND YOUR DAD DOESN'T
FIND OUT.'

ME
'HE LETS ME DO WHAT I
WANT. LEAST I'M NOT A
SWOT LIKE JESS.'

SUE
'I KNOW. MUST BE BORING
TO BE SOOO BRAINY.'

WHAT WOULD MUM SAY?

Once we send on a message, it goes out into cyberspace and
we lose control of it. It could be forwarded to someone
else, seen by other people on a friend's phone or stolen if
your account is hacked. The simplest thing is to make sure
your messages are polite, kind and wouldn't offend anyone.
A good rule of thumb for writing a message is: could you
show it to your mum? If not, don't send it to start with.

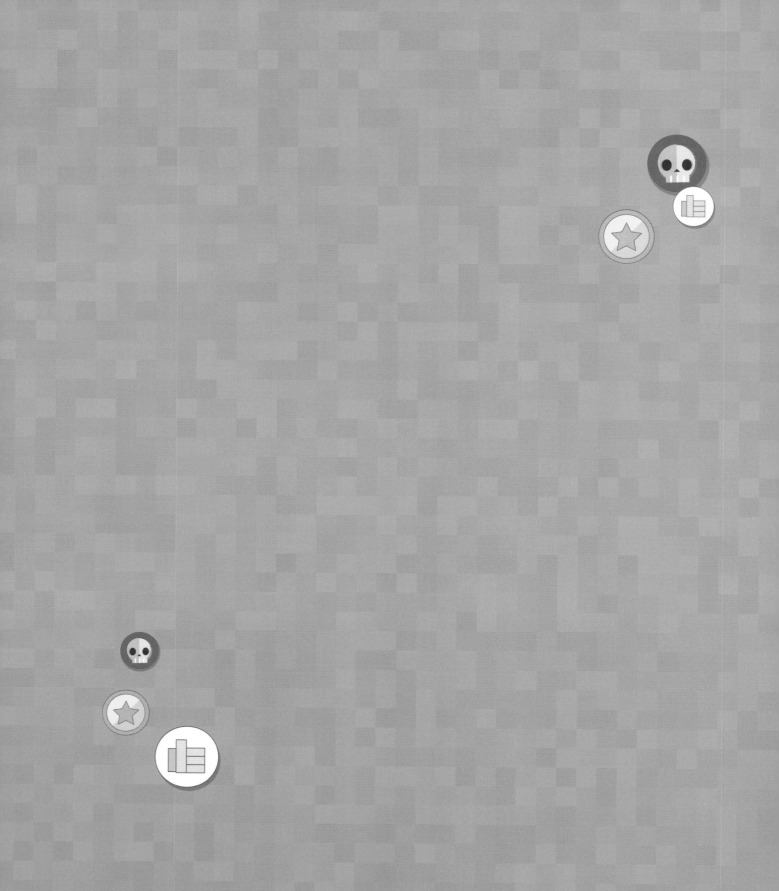

PROTECTING YOUR DEVICE

DIGITAL MAINTENANCE

Have you ever lost or broken your smartphone or tablet? It can be a bitter blow.

Sometimes, it's only when these devices are gone that we realise how much we use them. That's why smart digital citizens take care of their digital devices and keep them in good working order. These tips can show you how.

WHAT'S THAT YOU'VE GOT?

THIS IS A STEEL-REINFORCED, LEAD-LINED PROTECTION BOX FOR MY MOBILE. IT SHOULD NOW BE ABLE TO SURVIVE A NUCLEAR BLAST.

CASE PROTECTED

Buying a case for your digital device and a screen protector is a good, simple form of protection. These will keep your devices from becoming scratched and may save them from being broken if they are dropped.

SAFE STORAGE

Have a safe spot where you keep your digital device when it is not in use, such as a bookshelf. Keep your charger there too. This will keep your device from being sat or trodden on and also can help prevent you misplacing it.

PRESERVE YOUR BATTERY

Mobile batteries can last years if properly looked after. The best way of doing this is to charge them regularly. Experts say keeping your mobile battery at between 40 per cent and 80 per cent will greatly increase its life. A simpler tip is to try not to let your phone's battery drop below a 40 per cent charge.

DRY, NOT WET

It may seem obvious, but don't get your device wet by using it in the rain. Also be extra careful around open water, such as rivers, the sea and toilets!

IN SIGHT, OUT OF MIND

Never let your device out of sight when in public. Also make sure you have set a passcode on your device in case it ever gets stolen. This will prevent a thief accessing your information. You can even download anti-theft software to shut down and locate your phone if it is stolen. Ask your trusted adult for help with this.

UPDATE SOFTWARE

Carrying out software updates on your digital device can stop it being infected by viruses or malware. This is because software updates are often released soon after new harmful bugs and viruses have been detected. Software updates almost always improve your phone's performance too.

POP-UPS AND PITFALLS

All digital citizens know that the online world can be a mad maze of pop-up windows, flashing adverts and contest results.

Sometimes it's easy to click on the wrong thing and slip down a blind alleyway. To stay on the right path, beware of the following things.

I'VE WON A NEW PHONE! THEY JUST NEED MY PARENTS' CREDIT CARD DETAILS TO PAY FOR SHIPPING. IT'S WORTH IT!

CONTEST FAKERS

"Congratulations! You've won the latest phone!" When we see online adverts such as this, it seems too good to be true. That's because it is. If you click on the window it then asks you for your email address, postal address and sometimes your credit card number for shipping the prize. But these adverts are scams, so don't be fooled.

CLICKING THE RIGHT LINK

Often when we are looking to download the latest app or game, we click on the first link we see. But sometimes these downloads are fakes which can unleash harmful viruses or malware. Make sure you only download things from trusted websites that you have used before.

HIDDEN MOBILE CHARGES

Have you ever had a pop-up window on your phone wanting to predict your future or tell you which Star Wars character you are like? All that is needed is your smartphone number. However, by doing this and agreeing to the terms, you will almost certainly be charged a one-off fee. It's better to click away.

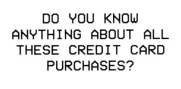

DO YOU KNOW ANYTHING ABOUT ALL THESE CREDIT CARD PURCHASES?

SOMEONE'S RIPPED US OFF. AND MY PHONE NEVER ARRIVED!

ACCIDENTAL SPENDING

It's easy to spend money online by accident. Some gaming apps are free to download, but charge to access a certain level. If your family uses an online store often and have their credit card details saved there, you can easily make a purchase by clicking on the wrong button. Use your common sense and read the terms and conditions to avoid these spending pitfalls.

VIRUSES AND MALWARE

Digital citizens have to protect their online accounts from cyber criminals and online scams, but they also have to protect their digital devices too.

This means preventing them being infected by harmful malware and viruses.

VIRUSES AND MALWARE

Some of the main programmes that can harm your digital devices are:

1   Malware: Short for MALicious SoftWARE, malware is designed to damage your device or steal the information that's on it.

STAY PROTECTED

The simplest defence against viruses and malware is not to click on any suspicious links or email attachments. You can create another line of defence by keeping your anti-virus software up to date. This is designed to stop dangerous programmes entering your digital device in the first place. Leaving your firewall switched on is also important. This is a security shield that stops scammers getting into your digital device.

FIENDISH FRIENDS?

Sometimes an email containing malware can be sent from a friend or family member's hacked account. These can come with attachments such as a greeting e-card that contains harmful malware. Be cautious of any emails with attachments and look out for spelling mistakes and anything else that looks fishy.

2 Virus:
Harmful malware that installs itself in the programmes on your digital device and spreads itself to other computers via the internet.

3 Spyware:
Malware that collects information about you from your digital device.

4 Trojan Horse:
A programme that gives someone secret access to your digital device, usually to steal from it.

THE LATEST THING

As consumers of new technology, digital citizens are often urged to 'buy, buy, buy'.

Technology companies constantly compete to release the latest gadget and their adverts insist we cannot do without it. An important part of being a digital citizen is understanding how to use today's technology. But how can we stay digitally literate without being pressured to purchase the 'latest thing'?

DON'T BELIEVE THE HYPE

Clever digital citizens know how to keep up-to-date with new technology without having to actually buy it. This is easily achieved by doing some research online. Reading online technology magazines and watching reviews of new gadgets is a great first step. This can keep you in the loop without having to spend money.

GREATEST, NOT LATEST

It's easy to see a new gadget advertised and fool ourselves into believing we can't live without it. However, with time this passes. After all, does your current gadget still work? Then why replace it? It's also important to realise the latest thing is not always the greatest thing. It's best to ignore our impulses to buy things and instead carefully evaluate what we need and what we don't. This is how clever digital citizens avoid being sucked into a never-ending buying loop.

PROTECTING YOURSELF AND OTHERS

CYBER STRANGERS

Online forums, gaming websites and chat rooms are great places to meet new people with similar interests to you.

However, unlike social media, everyone in these places is a stranger. This means you need to be extra careful around the people you meet, even if it feels like you quickly know them well.

MY AVATAR IS MASKGIRL. WHO ARE YOU?

I'M NINE. HOW OLD ARE YOU?

I'M CAPTAIN COOL! HOW OLD ARE YOU?

I'M NINE TOO!

STRANGER DANGER CHECKLIST

Dangerous cyber strangers are often very good at earning a child's trust. They can pretend to like all the same things as you and be interested in everything you say. Soon, they can seem like your best friend. But before long there will be some tell-tale signs that should set off some alarm bells. This is when you must tell your trusted adult what is going on. These signs can include:

1 Asking you questions about your school and local area.

WHO ARE YOU REALLY?

Because everyone you meet in an online forum or chat room has an avatar and screen name, you never know for sure who they really are. Someone who claims to be an eight-year-old girl from New York could be a 43-year-old man from London. Sometimes there are dangerous people online who wish to do children harm. That is why it's important not to give away any of your personal information.

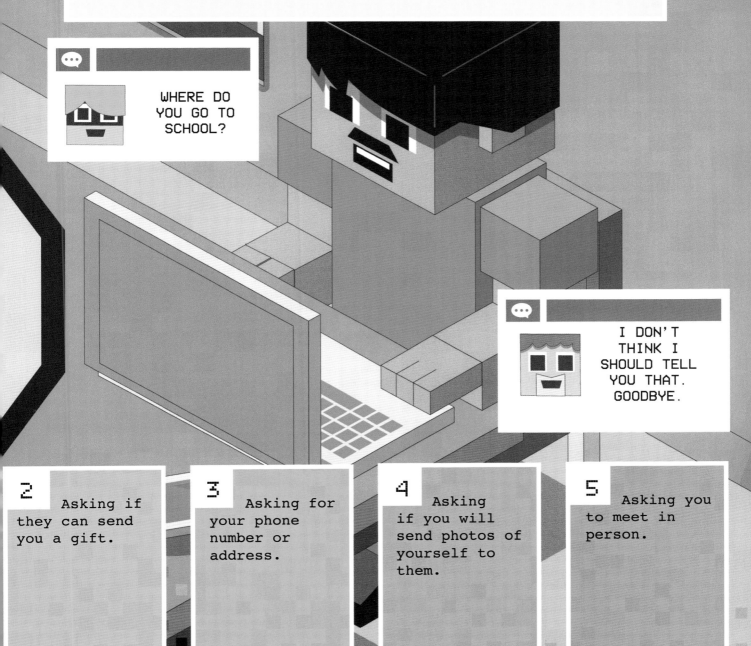

WHERE DO YOU GO TO SCHOOL?

I DON'T THINK I SHOULD TELL YOU THAT. GOODBYE.

2 Asking if they can send you a gift.

3 Asking for your phone number or address.

4 Asking if you will send photos of yourself to them.

5 Asking you to meet in person.

CYBER CRIMINALS

Cyber criminals are dishonest people who make money by scamming and stealing from others online.

Often, cyber criminals set a trap on the internet to catch out unsuspecting digital citizens. It can be easy to fall into these traps without even realising, so it's best to stay alert.

MAKE MONEY HERE

Adverts promising lots of money for little work often catch our attention. Who couldn't do with a bit more pocket money? Sometimes these adverts claim to be looking for child 'talent' for TV or film adverts. However, once you've joined they ask for money for agency 'fees'. It's simpler not to get sucked in to start with.

SPOT THE FAKE

It's not always easy to spot a real email or website from a fake. But the following are tell-tale signs to look out for:

BAD GRAMMAR AND SPELLING

Professional companies have editors that correct mistakes before something is posted online, but cyber criminals do not.

WEIRD-LOOKING LINKS

By resting your mouse (but not clicking) over a link, the real web address is shown. By comparing these, you can see if the link belongs to a fake website.

PHISHING EMAILS AND FAKE WEBSITES

Phishing means being sent an email containing a link that redirects you to a fake website. The website then asks you to download something, or enter your personal details or your credit card number. Your credit card can then be used illegally and the downloaded software can hack your computer and steal your personal information.

DID YOU GET THIS EMAIL FROM SCHOOL ASKING FOR YOUR DETAILS?

NO, THAT DOESN'T SOUND RIGHT. LET'S SEE.

LOOK, THEIR ADDRESS ISN'T QUITE RIGHT, THE EMAIL IS FULL OF SPELLING MISTAKES AND THIS LINK IS DODGY.

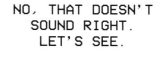

THIS IS A PHISHING EMAIL!

NO CONTACT DETAILS

Websites without street addresses and phone numbers are often fakes. You can also check a website's 'domain name' online to see if it is trustworthy or not. Your trusted adult can help you with this.

REQUESTS FOR DETAILS

Genuine websites and emails will never ask you for your bank PIN number or any other personal details that could be used to access your private life. Make sure these remain secret.

ONLINE SHOPPING

Shopping online is so popular that many people use it for almost all of their purchases.

It is possible to buy virtually anything online, but shopping this way can present some risks. Fake websites are a common danger. However, clever digital citizens know how to spot a fake website so they won't get scammed.

THIS ONE'S SUPER CHEAP.

PERHAPS IT'S TOO GOOD TO BE TRUE. DID YOU LOOK AT THE 'SPOT THE FAKE WEBSITE' CHECKLIST?

SPOT THE FAKE WEBSITE

You've found a website that offers the same products as elsewhere, but for much lower prices. Sound too good to be true? It probably is. Investigate the website by following this checklist:

1 Does it have broken English, spelling mistakes, or odd-sounding text?

2 Has the website's domain name been recently registered? Have a look by using a 'domain-name lookup'. Your trusted adult can help with this.

SPOT THE FAKE REVIEW

Sometimes fake websites post fake reviews to convince people that they are genuine. If there are a number of reviews that have been recently posted, this can be a sign that the reviews are fake. If the reviews are short, do not give much information and are all worded in the same way, this can be another tell-tale sign. If you find any such reviews about a website it is probably best to steer clear of it altogether.

MUM, YOU WERE RIGHT. THIS WEBSITE LOOKS LIKE A FAKE.

3 Does the website have any contact details, such as a phone number, street address or email address?

4 Is there a 'returns' page with a clear returns policy?

5 Has anyone had trouble with the website before? Check this out by dropping the website's name and the word 'review' or 'genuine?' into a search engine.
If the answers to any of these questions are 'yes', avoid it!

SPOT THE FAKE

In the modern world, digital citizens are often fed false news stories known as 'fake news'.

Fake news is written by people in order to mislead others. Some people publish fake news during elections to make their opponents look bad. Others do it for financial gain. Fake news can be dangerous when lots of people believe it to be true. However, it's easy to spot fake news by following the tips below.

DID YOU SEE A NEW PRESIDENT HAS BEEN ELECTED?

YES, THAT'S INTERESTING.

1. BEYOND THE HEADLINE

Fake news headlines often grab your attention by making bold statements and inserting exclamation marks. But by reading on, it often becomes quickly apparent the stories are not real.

2. WHAT'S THE SOURCE?

What website was the story published on originally? Is it a real website from a news organisation? Or is the web address simply made to look like it belongs to a real news organisation? Check the 'About' section to check if a website is a fake. If there are no contact details except a 'gmail' account, then it's probably fake.

3. CHECK THE AUTHOR

By typing the author's name into a search engine you can quickly uncover whether they are a real journalist, or even a real person.

4. SPELLING MISTAKES

Spelling mistakes and messy layouts are a dead giveaway that a news article or the website it is posted on has been created by an amateur.

5. CHECK SOURCES

Are real news organisations also reporting the news you are reading? Are people quoted in the story? Are these quotes real, and are they real people? It's easy to find out by doing an online search on the quotes, the names and the news itself. If the search engine results only lead you back to the same article, it's a good sign that it's a fake.

6. NEWS OR ADVERT?

Sometimes advertisements are dressed up to look like news stories and used on a real news site. These are not 'fake news', but it's easy to mistake them for real news. Often they have an 'advertisement' or 'sponsored content' label to warn you they are not news, but not always.

FREE SPEECH

Free speech is one of any citizen's central rights, including digital citizens.

This means not being scared to say what you think when you post a comment, message or blog online. However, it doesn't mean being able to say anything at all. In the online world people need to respect others and their opinions, even if they disagree with them.

WHAT IS FREE SPEECH?

Free speech is a recognised human right according to international law. It gives people the right to express themselves without interference. This important right was partly won during the 18th century French and American revolutions, when people rose up against their rulers.

FREE SPEECH GONE BAD

Freedom of speech is not covered by law when people say rude or hurtful things about others. This is especially true when attacks are made against people because of their skin colour, sexuality, religion or country of origin. These are known as hate crimes and are taken very seriously by the police.

RESPECTING OPINIONS

The online world is a free place where people should give their opinions openly and respect the right of others to have different opinions. As long as they are not hurting others, different opinions are what make both the real and online worlds such interesting places.

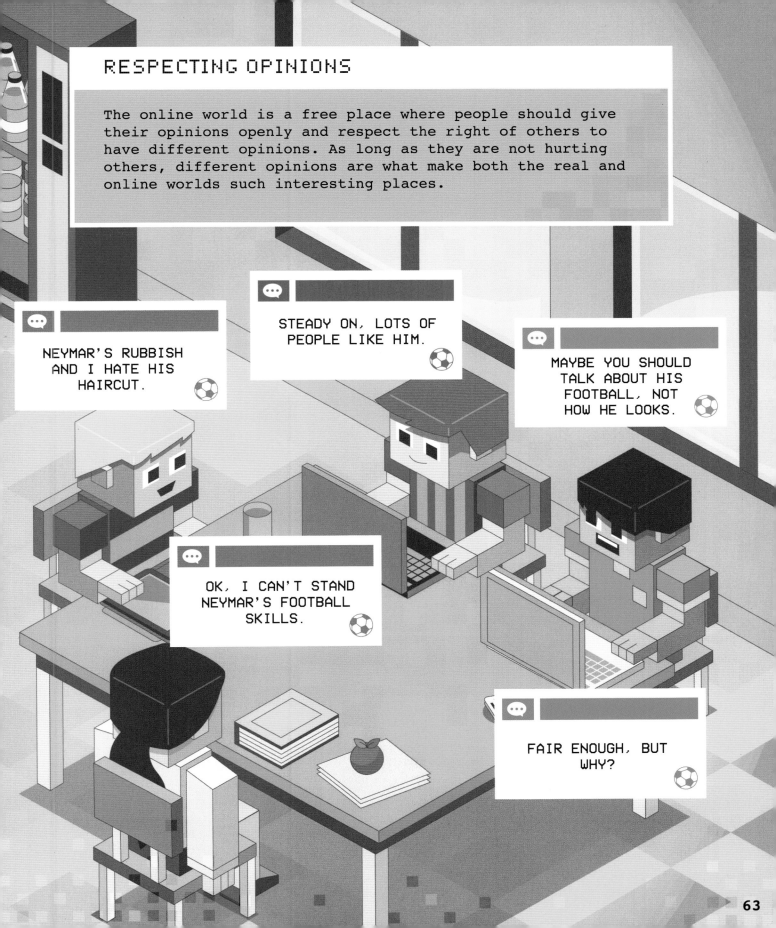

NEYMAR'S RUBBISH AND I HATE HIS HAIRCUT.

STEADY ON, LOTS OF PEOPLE LIKE HIM.

MAYBE YOU SHOULD TALK ABOUT HIS FOOTBALL, NOT HOW HE LOOKS.

OK, I CAN'T STAND NEYMAR'S FOOTBALL SKILLS.

FAIR ENOUGH, BUT WHY?

DIGITAL LAW

Digital law is designed to protect digital citizens against online crime.

Online crime can include identity theft, illegal downloading and bullying. However, every country has different laws about online crime and there is no international police force looking after the internet. That is why if you see something you think is harmful or wrong, it is always a good idea to report it to a trusted adult.

HARASSMENT AND BULLYING

While many countries agree that online bullying is a crime, not all agree on what should be done about it. When online bullying happens among children, often the local police work in conjunction with the school. Those found guilty can be expelled from the school or prosecuted under harassment laws. The simplest thing is to tell a trusted adult if it is happening to you or someone you know.

EWWW! SOMEONE HAS PUT HORRIBLE PICTURES ALL OVER MY WALL.

COME ON, LET'S TELL MY DAD.

WHAT ARE ONLINE CRIMES?

The following are typical online crimes:

1 Hacking into websites

2 Stealing someone's information or identity

3 Illegal file sharing

DEFAMATION

Telling lies about someone is a crime known as defamation. Defamation can be something that is written, known as libel, or something that is spoken, known as slander. Defamation is very serious if somebody tells lies that damage a person's reputation. If someone is found guilty of this crime, they often have to pay a lot of money to the person they defamed.

ORIGINAL ONLINE WORK

Can you imagine if you wrote an essay, article or book that somebody then claimed was their work?

This is what it is like for people who have their work plagiarised. Under copyright law, it is illegal to pretend to have created something that you have not. This includes using someone else's writing for school essays and homework.

> JULIE, I NEED TO SEE YOU ABOUT YOUR ASSIGNMENT.

CITING SOURCES

Often when we are doing research we find a writer has summed up something so well that we wish we had written it ourselves. It's okay to use a writer's exact words if you get permission to do so and then attribute the text to them. This is called 'citing your sources'. You can ask your teacher how to cite sources in your homework and essays.

ESSAYS AND HOMEWORK

It's easy to cut and paste a sentence from a webpage and then drop it into your own essay or homework assignment. It may not seem serious, but doing so is plagiarising someone else's work. In serious cases, students have handed in whole essays that they have copied directly from the internet. It's not difficult to find out if something has been plagiarised and it can get that person into a lot of trouble.

I REALLY LIKED YOUR ESSAY, BUT THERE WERE SOME SENTENCES THAT YOU PASTED STRAIGHT FROM THE INTERNET.

I THOUGHT ONE SENTENCE HERE AND THERE WAS OK.

IT WOULD BE IF YOU ATTRIBUTED THE SENTENCES TO THE ORIGINAL AUTHOR. LET ME SHOW YOU HOW TO DO THAT.

ILLEGAL DOWNLOADS

It might seem like lots of people download music, films and games for free these days.

However, downloading any material that is under copyright is stealing and is therefore against the law. Copyright law applies to everyone, no matter what age they are. That means anyone that illegally downloads files could get into trouble.

LOOK, EVEN THE NEW LEGO MOVIE IS ON HERE.

YOU'RE SURE WE WON'T GET INTO TROUBLE?

AWESOME, I'M GETTING IT TONIGHT.

I DON'T KNOW, IT SEEMS DODGY.

WHAT IS COPYRIGHT?

When somebody creates something, such as a book, song or films they own it under copyright. This means they get to decide what happens to it. To use the work, people normally have to seek the copyright-holder's permission and pay a fee. This stops people stealing the work of others. It also means if you download something which is under copyright for free, you are breaking the law.

ILLEGAL DOWNLOADING

There are many legal websites where you can pay a fee to download films, songs or books. Then there are other illegal websites that offer these files for free. By using these sites, people are not only breaking the law but also run the risk of downloading a file that contains harmful malware or viruses. Often the quality of the files can also be very poor. It is best to avoid these websites and file-sharing altogether, even if it is tempting to get something for nothing.

I DOWNLOADED THAT MOVIE, BUT THE SOUND IS RUBBISH.

PHEW! GLAD I DIDN'T JOIN IN.

AND MY LAPTOP STARTED ACTING WEIRDLY AFTERWARDS.

YEAH, ME TOO. I'M SORRY.

LOOKING AFTER YOUR MIND

APP ATTACK

Twenty years ago, people mainly sat at desktop computers to go online.

Back then, the internet was brand new and some people said it would never catch on! Now, the internet is part of everyday life and our smartphones keep us constantly connected wherever we go. These digital devices can make us feel in control — but are they controlling us? Smart digital citizens look after their mental health as much as their physical health.

PICK UP THAT PHONE?

A smartphone is a great tool, but also something to look at when you don't know what else to do. How much time do you spend randomly picking up your phone? Why not try a diary experiment? For one day, write down each time you pick up your phone, how long you use it for and what you do on it. There are apps that do this too. When you look at the results, ask yourself: 'How much of this time was well spent?'

THE ANTI APPS

If you think you are picking up your digital device too often, you could try one of the following activities. These 'Anti Apps' will help you to fill your time differently.

1 Write a letter. Use a pen and paper and send the letter in an envelope. Your gran will be amazed!

2 Draw a picture. Use pens, pencils and paper and don't check the internet for inspiration.

I FEEL AWFUL!

Sometimes being online can make us feel confused, anxious or depressed. We can see things that upset us or read things that make us feel bad about ourselves. Looking after your mental health is a very important aspect of being a digital citizen. If you are experiencing any of the above things, then it's important to talk to someone. Your trusted adult is a great place to start. There are also phone helplines where you can talk to experts anonymously. Most of all, this is a good time to take a break from the online world.

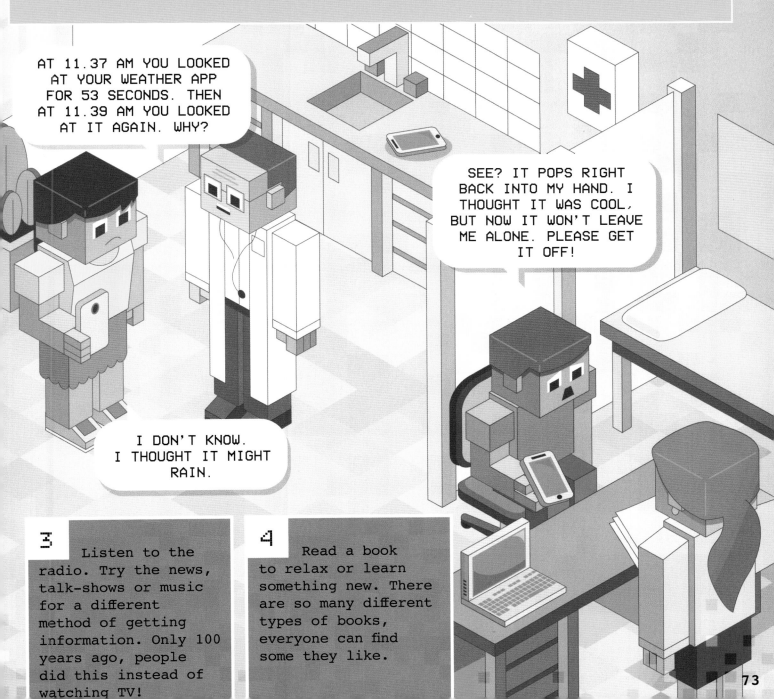

AT 11.37 AM YOU LOOKED AT YOUR WEATHER APP FOR 53 SECONDS. THEN AT 11.39 AM YOU LOOKED AT IT AGAIN. WHY?

SEE? IT POPS RIGHT BACK INTO MY HAND. I THOUGHT IT WAS COOL, BUT NOW IT WON'T LEAVE ME ALONE. PLEASE GET IT OFF!

I DON'T KNOW. I THOUGHT IT MIGHT RAIN.

3 Listen to the radio. Try the news, talk-shows or music for a different method of getting information. Only 100 years ago, people did this instead of watching TV!

4 Read a book to relax or learn something new. There are so many different types of books, everyone can find some they like.

ONLINE ADDICTION

For some digital citizens, spending too much time online leads to more serious problems.

They can become addicted to the digital world and find it difficult to do anything else. Sometimes, they give up seeing other people and become isolated and alone. When this happens, they often need help to get better.

MADDY? WE'D LIKE TO TALK TO YOU.

MADDY'S ROOM

GO AWAY!

I HAVEN'T SEEN YOU IN DAYS!

AM I ADDICTED?

There is a big difference between spending lots of time online and being addicted. However, if you experience the following signs it is best to talk to your trusted adult about it:

1 You spend all of your spare time online and sacrifice sleep to be on it.

2 You become angry, irritated or depressed when you are not online.

THE REWARD FEELING

The online world can make us feel good in lots of ways. On social media, we look forward to receiving comments about our posts and then feel rewarded when people 'like' them. Finishing a difficult level in an online game can give us a rewarding buzz too. Some people want to feel the excitement the internet provides over and over again, until they become addicted to it.

3 You disobey time limits set for being online and lie about it.

4 You prefer to be online than spend time with friends or family.

5 Your school work is suffering and you ignore other commitments to be online.

SOCIAL MEDIA AND SELF-IMAGE

Social media is one of our favourite ways of staying in touch with friends and family.

With our smartphones we can instantly snap a selfie and upload it in seconds. While we wait for comments, we can check out what our friends have posted too. However, sometimes this can make us feel bad about ourselves. It can seem like other people have more friends and are having a better time than us.

LIKE THE HUMAN

Often the best social media posts are of people looking silly, making a mistake or laughing at themselves. This is because they are celebrating being human and sharing it with others. This is much more fun than posting perfect photos, or writing about our exciting lives. So the next time you slip over or spill soup down your front, post a picture of it and see what kind of responses come in.

BEST FACE FORWARD

Clever digital citizens remember that social media is not a true reflection of the real world. That is because most people only post pictures of themselves looking good and some retouch or digitally alter the photos first. The same is often true of people's activities. Some people's social media accounts make their lives seem action-packed and amazing. But that's because nobody posts images of themselves getting up in the morning, or doing up their shoelaces. It's important to remember that nobody's life is always interesting or without problems.

JAMES HAS MUCH BETTER FRIENDS THAN ME AND IS ALWAYS DOING COOL STUFF WITH THEM.

AVOIDING ADVERTS

Have you ever noticed how many advertisements there are online?

Adverts are crammed into every nook and cranny: flashing and popping up at us and enticing us to click on them. They promise us beauty, success and happiness if we buy their products. However, clever digital citizens know not to believe them.

ADVERTS AND MARKETING

Marketing is how adverts target particular groups to sell them things. That is why many adverts are aimed at kids. Marketers often call children under the age of 12 'pesterers'. This is because they don't have much money of their own, but often pester their parents to buy them the 'latest thing'. Marketers promise the latest thing will make us happy, but the latest thing is soon replaced by another latest thing. Smart digital citizens know that buying products can bring a few moments of pleasure, but it cannot provide us with long-term happiness.

NOT NEWS

Have you ever clicked on a news story online just to find out it is actually an advert? This is one way clever advertisers trick us into reading about their products. Sometimes these adverts in disguise are labelled 'sponsored content', 'promoted' or 'advertisement'. However, when they are not labelled we need to keep our wits about us and pause before clicking on them.

BEING BOYS AND GIRLS

The online world is full of images and advice about how we should look and act as girls and boys.

These are known as gender stereotypes. Gender stereotypes often tell us that girls should be pretty, polite and ladylike, while boys should be tough, athletic and never cry. Smart digital citizens do not buy into gender stereotypes. Instead they promote an equal online world, where people are allowed to be themselves.

WOAH. LOOK AT THAT GUY. I WISH I WERE LIKE HIM.

SHE LOOKS SO PERFECT!

THE MALE AND FEMALE MODEL

Online adverts, celebrity websites and fashion e-zines like to show us models with toned bodies, beautiful hair and perfect smiles. These can make us feel bad about the way we look. However, it's important to remember these images have nothing to do with the real world. Most people do not look like models and many online photos of models have been heavily retouched and digitally altered before being published.

BREAK THE MOULD

The online world shows us many gender stereotypes, but it is also a great place to fight against them. Boys and girls can use male or female avatars and screen names, or choose ones that are unisex, for example. It is also a great place to educate people that stereotypes make the world a more narrow-minded place. After all, there are lots of athletic girls and polite boys and everyone is allowed to cry!

YEAH BUT LOOK, I FOUND THE UNALTERED VERSION. THIS IS WHAT THEY REALLY LOOK LIKE!

DIGITAL TOLERANCE

Good digital citizens believe in a tolerant world where people can be what they want. This includes boys who like dressing as girls. It can also include girls and boys who feel like they were born as the wrong gender and want to swap. Called the trans-gender community, these people have a big presence on the internet. This helps others understand who they are and helps to eliminate prejudices people may have against them.

CYBERBULLIES AND TROLLS

Cyberbullies and trolls are internet users that say mean things about others and harass them online.

Often they post nasty comments, or photos, or send the victim cruel messages. Both trolls and cyberbullies should be taken very seriously so the problem doesn't get worse.

YOUR AVATAR SUCKS. YOU'RE AN IDIOT.

CYBERBULLIES

A cyberbully is often someone we know who has decided to pick on us. It is important to tell your trusted adult straight away if this happens to you. They may choose to get in touch with your school, the website where the abuse is happening and sometimes the police. Remember that you are not to blame for the bullying.

TROLLS

Online trolls are usually people we don't know who have decided to launch a random attack online. They often lie in wait in forums or chat rooms before making nasty comments and posting rude photographs. Sometimes an attack by a troll can seem silly and like no big deal. But trolling is a form of cyberbullying and should always be reported. After you have done so, it is best to follow the 'Ignore, block and unfollow' rule. Trolls usually go away when they do not get attention.

DON'T DO IT. REMEMBER: 'IGNORE, BLOCK AND UNFOLLOW.' THEN LET'S TELL DAD.

HOW DARE THEY SAY THAT! I'LL TELL THEM WHAT I THINK!

DOXXING

Doxxing is when a cyberbully posts the personal details of their victim so other people can bully them too. This sometimes involves hacking into the victim's online accounts to steal their details. This is why having strong passwords is so important.

BYSTANDING

Part of being a good digital citizen is protecting other people from being bullied online.

Some people say 'it's not my problem' and watch this type of harassment continue. Others step in to support the person being bullied.

BYSTANDERS

A bystander is someone who watches something bad happening, but does nothing to help. When cyberbullying takes place, a bystander says it is none of their business or that they can't be bothered to get involved.

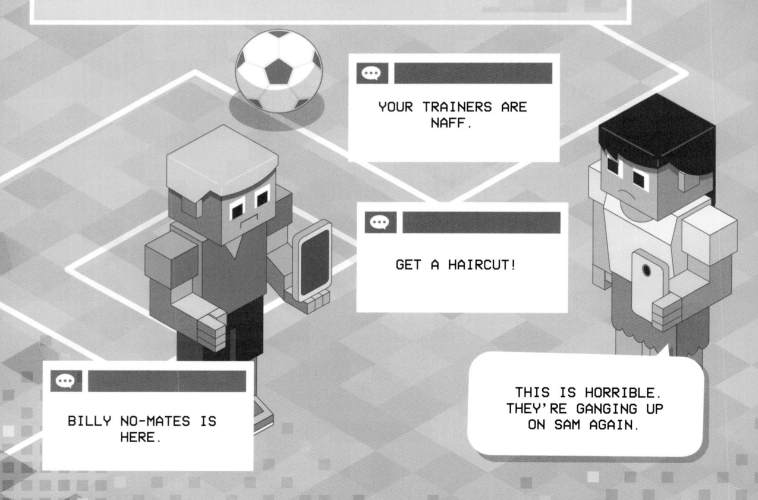

YOUR TRAINERS ARE NAFF.

GET A HAIRCUT!

BILLY NO-MATES IS HERE.

THIS IS HORRIBLE. THEY'RE GANGING UP ON SAM AGAIN.

UPSTANDERS

Upstanders are people who step in to show their support for a victim of cyberbullying. They report the abuse to a trusted adult, their school, the social media site where it is happening and sometimes the police. Just letting the bullied person know you are on their side can also make a huge difference.

PEER PRESSURE

Sometimes cyberbullies encourage others to join in and pick on someone together. This often means forwarding or 'liking' nasty online messages about the victim, or passing on their online details so others can bully them too. This is peer pressure and it can make life unbearable for the person being picked on. When this happens the role of an upstander is more important than ever.

I'VE JUST SEEN SOME OF THE MESSAGES BEING POSTED. ARE YOU OK?

WHOEVER SENT THESE IS A COWARD.

INFORMATION INVASION

The internet is a free resource and we should all have the freedom to seek and receive information from it.

However, sometimes websites that are harmful or inappropriate for children are blocked. You can ask a teacher or parent to explain why you have been blocked from using certain websites. Digital citizens should be allowed to ask about online rules so they can understand why they are obeying them.

WHY CAN'T I OPEN THE NASA WEBSITE TODAY?

AND I CAN'T VISIT NATIONAL GEOGRAPHIC ANYMORE!

FILTERS

Internet filters are put in place to block websites with particular content, such as sex or violence. These websites aren't good for children and can be confusing or upsetting. However, sometimes filters also block helpful websites by mistake. If you think something has been blocked incorrectly, point it out to a parent or teacher.

WHICH WEBSITES ARE HARMFUL?

Websites that are definitely harmful are those which promote hatred or violence towards others. Websites with adult themes such as sex or violence are also not appropriate for children. Websites that ask for your personal information should always be avoided. However, a simple rule of thumb is: if you see anything that you don't like on a website, just click out.

EXCUSE ME SIR, WE CAN'T ACCESS OUR FAVOURITE SITES.

OUR NEW CONTENT FILTERS MUST HAVE BLOCKED THEM BY ACCIDENT. I'LL GET THIS FIXED.

LOOKING AFTER YOUR BODY

PREPARE TO PREVENT PAIN

The human body has evolved over hundreds of thousands of years to carry out physical tasks. We were not designed for sitting in front of a computer making small, repetitive movements for hours on end. To perform this relatively new work we must look after our bodies and help them adjust.

REPETITIVE STRAIN INJURY

A repetitive strain injury is a painful condition that usually affects the hands, wrists and arms. It is caused by repeating small movements over and over again, and therefore often affects computer users. Its symptoms include stiffness, tingling, numbness and burning sensations. It's important that if you feel any of these symptoms you limit using your digital devices and talk to a doctor as soon as possible. Repetitive strain injuries are treatable, but it's best to prevent them happening in the first place.

SITTING STRAIGHT

How we sit at a computer is the first step in preventing pain and physical problems. Follow these five easy steps to set up your work station correctly:

1
Support your back with a chair that keeps your spine straight and not hunched. This is called good posture.

2
Position the screen to eye level so you are not bending your neck to look at it.

3 Keep your legs bent at a right angle, with your feet flat on a footrest or the ground.

4 Keep your arms at a right angle to the desk, so you are not reaching up or down to type.

5 Make sure your hands and wrists are straight and not bent while using the keyboard and mouse.

STRETCH, DON'T STRAIN

Have you ever noticed how you hold your body when you are concentrating on something online?

Often we make our limbs rigid, hunch up our shoulders and even clench our jaws. Without even realising it we are making ourselves tense and tight. This is very bad for our bodies. Clever digital citizens take micro-breaks to stretch their muscles and relax.

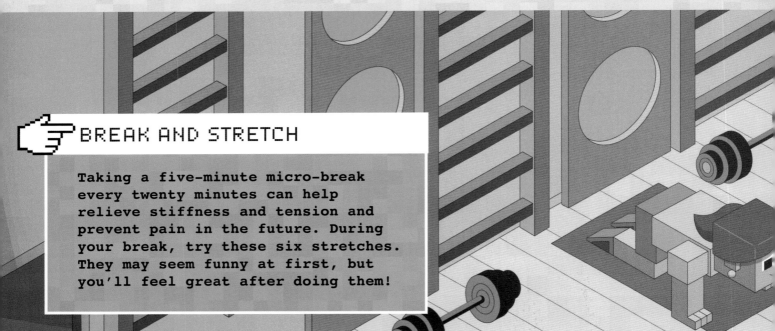

BREAK AND STRETCH

Taking a five-minute micro-break every twenty minutes can help relieve stiffness and tension and prevent pain in the future. During your break, try these six stretches. They may seem funny at first, but you'll feel great after doing them!

1 Stretch your fingers out straight, hold for ten seconds, then relax. Now bend your fingers at the knuckles, hold for ten seconds, then relax.

2 Raise your eyebrows, open your eyes and mouth wide and stick out your tongue for ten seconds. Try not to laugh. Then relax.

3 Raise your shoulders slowly up to your ears, hold for five seconds, then relax.

AVOID EYESTRAIN

With all that time spent staring at screens, digital citizens need to look after their eye health. A simple exercise is to look away from the screen every twenty minutes and concentrate on something in the distance for twenty seconds or so. This helps relax the eye muscles and prevent eye strain. Also remember to blink often!

WHAT ARE YOU DOING?

YOGA. WE'RE PREPARING FOR A HARDCORE GAMING SESSION.

4	5	6
Lock your fingers behind your head and pull your shoulder blades gently together. Hold for ten seconds, then relax.	Slowly tilt your head to one side, hold for ten seconds, then straighten and relax. Now do the same on the other side.	Slowly turn your chin towards your left shoulder, hold for ten seconds, then relax. Now do the same for the other side.
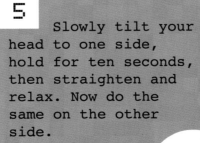		

DIGITAL TRAINING

Has an adult ever told you that a healthy body leads to a healthy mind?

It may sound boring, but it is actually true. Smart digital citizens train to be online by doing some physical exercise every day and getting enough sleep. This keeps their brains sharp and their bodies in shape for every internet adventure.

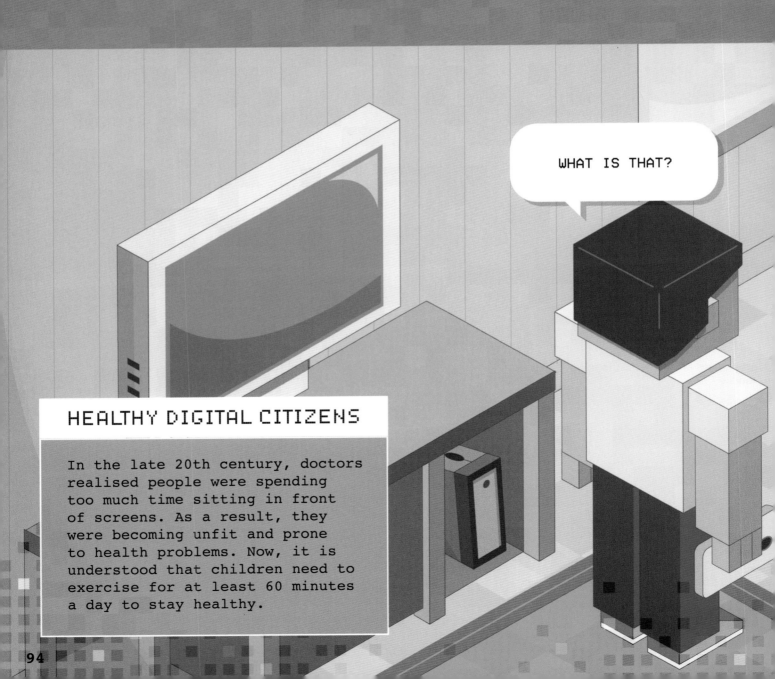

WHAT IS THAT?

HEALTHY DIGITAL CITIZENS

In the late 20th century, doctors realised people were spending too much time sitting in front of screens. As a result, they were becoming unfit and prone to health problems. Now, it is understood that children need to exercise for at least 60 minutes a day to stay healthy.

EXERCISE NOW

It's easy to put off doing exercise when you are online. There's always a message to finish, a website to browse or a level to conquer. Before you know it, it's time to have dinner or go to bed. But it's also easy to stand up and do some exercise, such as a run, a bike ride or a walk. Setting an alarm to do this is a good way to remind yourself.

SWITCH OFF BEFORE SLEEP

Did you know that staring at a screen before bedtime is like running a race and then trying to sleep? Turning all your digital devices off at least an hour before bedtime is the best way of winding down and getting a proper night's rest. The online world will still be there in the morning.

I'M IN TROUBLE

Even the most careful digital citizens can sometimes make mistakes online.

This can include accidentally giving too much away about ourselves to someone we don't really know. We may have told them some of our personal information, sent them photos or made them a promise we don't want to keep. It's important to remember that it's never too late to tell your trusted adult if anything like this has happened. It's also important to never do something you don't want to do for someone — even if they are putting pressure on you.

I THINK WE SHOULD MEET FOR REAL.

IF YOU DON'T, I'M GOING TO GET YOU IN TROUBLE.

I'LL SHOW YOUR PARENTS THAT PHOTO YOU SENT OF YOURSELF.

STOP THE STRANGER

Dangerous cyber strangers often pressure their victims and can even threaten them to get what they want. If this is happening to you, remember that you have the power to stop anything more happening. Follow these steps to make things better:

1 Tell your trusted adult what has happened. Be honest about what has taken place: they are there to help you.

2 If you don't feel like there is a trusted adult you want to tell, you can call a helpline just for kids. Your call will be private and not shared with anyone else. Some useful numbers are on page 111 of this book.

3 Make a record of all of your correspondence with the stranger, including screen shots. This will help your trusted adult and police investigate. Then block the stranger from all of your accounts.

4 Pat yourself on the back for asking for help. You have done the right thing and started taking back control of your life. Remember that you should never be ashamed to ask for help — regardless of what has happened.

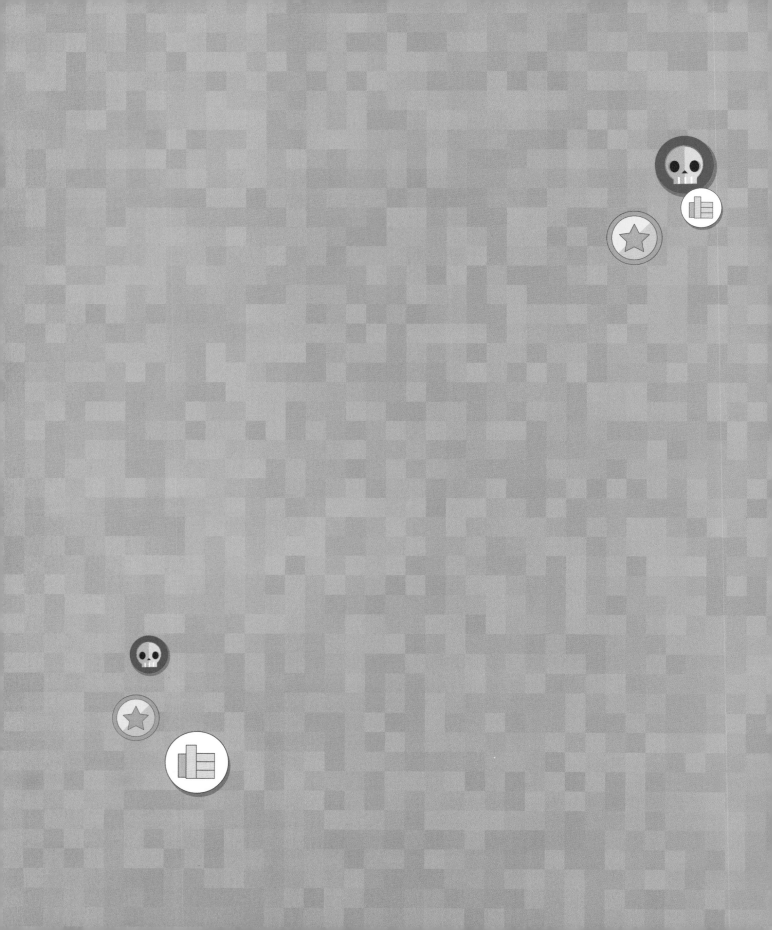

A DIGITAL WORLD FOR EVERYBODY

UNITING ONLINE

The online world is a great way of uniting people from small communities and minorities in the real world.

They may be people from different ethnic or religious backgrounds, or those with special needs or alternative lifestyles. By finding others like themselves online, those who feel alone or on the outside of society can be more included.

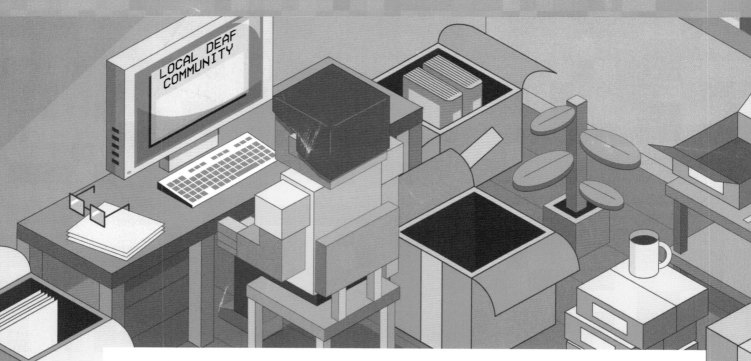

SPECIAL NEEDS

The internet can be an empowering tool for those with special needs. Texting and messaging apps are a helpful technology for deaf people, for example. Before the internet, deaf people had to rely on fax machines instead of telephones for fast, long distance communication. This is one way internet technologies can help everyone participate more easily in our society.

MINORITY MILLIONS

The real world is made up of millions of different minorities. Minorities are those from groups that are different from mainstream society. These groups can have various religious, ethnic or cultural backgrounds. They may have a different sexual orientation or gender identity, such as those from the lesbian, gay, bisexual or transgender (LGBT) communities. People from minority groups can feel isolated and be discriminated against. However, social media can help them connect with each other and become more visible to the world. This helps fight against intolerance.

LOOK ISLA, THERE IS A LOCAL GROUP FOR DEAF PEOPLE LIKE US HERE.

SEEKING SUPPORT

It's easy to find a support group online if you need one. Maybe you've broken a leg and want to reach out to others who are also laid up. Maybe you've been suffering from a bad illness, or are just feeling down. Finding other people who are in the same position as you can make you feel much better. Otherwise it can be easy to feel alone.

EDUCATING THE WORLD

Clever digital citizens want to live in a world of online users who can use technology well.

This means helping other people to use their digital devices. Many older people were not surrounded by online technology when they were growing up. This means they can sometimes need younger people to help them.

LET ME SHOW YOU HOW TO USE IT, DAD.

BE A GOOD DIGITAL TEACHER

The followings tips can help you become a good digital teacher, even with adults that can't use their digital devices properly!

DON'T ASSUME

Some people have never heard of social media or mobile apps! If you're showing someone how to do something online, don't assume they will understand what any of the names mean.

GETTING THE BASICS

If you're showing someone how to do something online, just teach them the basics first. Otherwise it's easy for them to get overwhelmed. Once they've got it, you can show them more.

PRAISE IS GOOD

Even adults need to be told that they are doing a good job sometimes! Saying things like 'That's good' and 'You've got it' can make a big difference.

BE PATIENT

Everyone learns in different ways, so it's important not to get irritated if someone doesn't understand something straight away.

KEEP LEARNING

There's always more to learn about online technology and smart digital citizens make sure they are up-to-date with what's new. Never feel afraid to ask someone about new technology.

ACCESS FOR ALL

Today, digital technology is all around us.

We use this technology to learn, have fun and message our friends. Surely everyone in the world must own at least one digital device, such as a laptop, tablet or smartphone — right? That's not actually the case. In many places, children don't own any digital devices. Others don't have access to the internet at all.

YOUR TURN IN 15 MINUTES.

A WORLD OF OPPORTUNITY

Good digital citizens believe that everyone should have online access, regardless of who they are, where they live and how much money they have. No one should miss out on the amazing opportunities the online world can offer.

HOW CAN I HELP?

There are lots of ways you can help bring internet access to those without it, both in your own community and beyond. Here are a few of them:

RECYCLE OLD DEVICES

Ask your teacher if your school can set up a recycling box for old, unwanted digital devices. These phones, tablets and computers can go to less fortunate people in your area, or abroad.

FUNDRAISERS FOR FACILITIES

Holding a fundraiser, such as a bake sale, can help your school buy digital devices for your school library or computer room, or to lend out to pupils. Ask your teacher about organising one.

ASK YOUR PARENTS

Adults can be helpful sometimes because they know lots of other adults. Ask your parents if they know any businesses that would donate money or digital devices to your school. They might be happy to help when they find out what you're doing.

DIGITAL DETOX

The online world is a fast-moving place that never sleeps.

You can have instant communication with others, play games around the clock and browse websites at any time of day or night. No wonder that digital citizens can feel a little frazzled at times. When you feel like this it's a good idea to give yourself a digital detox.

SORRY, I'M READING MY BOOK.

DO YOU KNOW WHAT THE WI-FI LOG IN IS HERE?

TURN OFF AND TUNE IN

Taking a digital detox means switching off all your devices and giving your brain a break. This is a great time to visit a friend in person. It helps you remember real humans are fun, friendly and have flaws, unlike the edited versions they can post on their social media accounts.

FANTASY VS REALITY

Online gaming is great entertainment, but sometimes it can be hard to shake a game off. If you find yourself walking down a street imagining jumping over cars, hurling grenades, or driving rally cars, perhaps you are suffering from gaming overload. Thankfully, the real world is a much calmer and more ordered place. Remember to enjoy it too.

NON DIGITAL CITIZENS

When we're online, it's easy to imagine that the whole world is online too. But it isn't. There are billions of people in the world who don't have a digital device or an internet connection. Many of them live around us. It's nice to remember that being a digital citizen is not essential to having a fulfilling life. After all, the greatest experiences in life happen in the real world, not the online one.

GLOSSARY

Addiction
Feeling physically and mentally dependent on having something.

Apps
Short for 'applications', apps are computer programmes for mobile digital devices, such as smartphones or tablets.

Attachment
A file, such as a picture or word document, sent as part of an email.

Avatar
A computer icon or image that people use to represent themselves online.

Block
A way of stopping someone from sending you nasty messages, emails or texts online.

Carbon footprint
The amount of harmful carbon dioxide that is released into the atmosphere as a result of one person's activities.

Crowdfund
When a lot of people each contribute a sum of money to pay for a project.

Cyberbullying
Bullying that takes place online or using internet-based apps.

Detox
Taking a break from something that is done often and may have harmful effects.

Digital
Technology that involves computers.

Download
To take information or files from the internet and store them on your computer.

Etiquette
The rules for behaving politely in society.

Hack
To break into computers and computer networks online.

Hacker
A computer expert who breaks into computers and computer networks online.

Instant messaging
Apps that allow for text messages to be sent via the internet.

Internet
The vast electronic network that allows billions of computers from around the world to connect to each other.

Malware
A dangerous computer programme that is created to damage or disable other digital devices.

Microblogging
A social media post, usually under 300 characters that can have images, videos, links and audio clips attached.

Online
Being connected to the internet via a computer or digital device.

Passcode
A password made up of numbers or letters that prevents access to your digital device.

Predator
A dangerous person who searches for others to harm.

Search engine
A computer programme that carries out a search of available information on the internet based on the words you type in.

Selfie
Taking a photo of oneself, often using a smartphone and sometimes a 'selfie' stick.

Sexuality
A person's sexual feelings, whether they are attracted to a person of a different sex or the same sex.

Smartphone
A mobile phone that is capable of connecting to the internet.

Social media
Websites that allow users to share content and information online

Stereotype
An oversimplified view of somebody held by many people.

Trusted adult
An adult you know well and trust.

Upload
Transferring something from your computer or digital device onto the internet.

Virtual reality (VR)
Computer-generated environment that people can interact with.

Virus
A dangerous program that can 'infect' a computer, destroying the information it holds.

Website
A collection of web pages that is stored on a computer and made available to people over the internet.

HELPFUL WEBSITES

Digital citizenship

The following websites have helpful information about digital citizenship for young people:

www.digizen.org/kids/

www.digitalcitizenship.nsw.edu.au

www.cyberwise.org/digitalcitizenship-games

www.digitalcitizenship.net/nine-elements.html

Bullying

These websites have excellent advice for kids who are experiencing bullying online. There are also some helplines which children can call anonymously to receive expert advice:

www.childline.org.uk/info-advice/bullying-abuse-safety/types-bullying/bullying-cyberbullying/

Childline helpline for kids: 0800 1111

www.bullying.co.uk

BullyingUK helpline for kids: 0808 800 2222

www.stopbullying.gov/kids/facts/

www.commonsensemedia.org/videos/5-ways-to-stop-cyberbullies-0

Staying safe

These websites are dedicated to keeping kids safe online, with lots of good advice:

www.childnet.com/young-people/primary/get-smart

www.kidsmart.org.uk

www.safetynetkids.org.uk/personal-safety/staying-safe-online/

www.bbc.co.uk/newsround/

INDEX

Franklin Watts
First published in Great Britain in 2021 by
The Watts Publishing Group
Copyright © The Watts Publishing
Group 2021

All rights reserved.

Editor: Julia Bird
Illustrator: Diego Vaisberg
Packaged by: Collaborate

ISBN 978 1 4451 7291 0 (hb)
     978 1 4451 7292 7 (pb)

Every attempt has been made to clear copyright.
Should there be any inadvertent omission please
apply to the publisher for rectification.

Franklin Watts
An imprint of
Hachette Children's Group
Part of The Watts Publishing Group
Carmelite House
50 Victoria Embankment
London EC4Y 0DZ

An Hachette UK Company
www.hachette.co.uk
www.franklinwatts.co.uk
Printed in Dubai

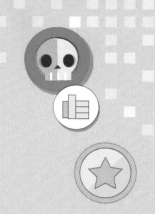

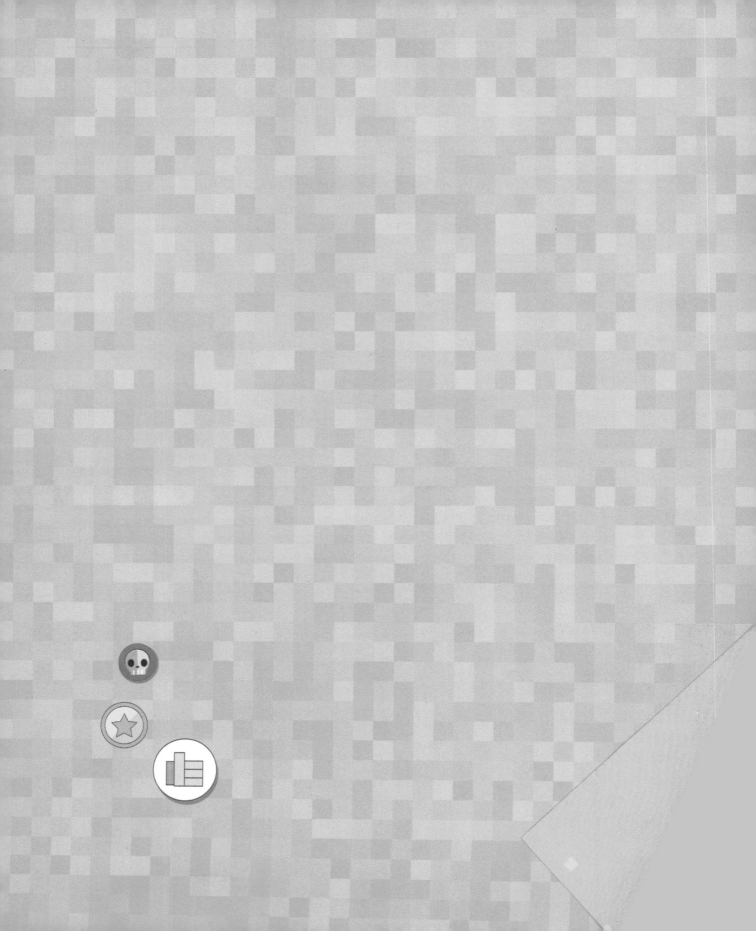